CUBA

A TRUE BOOK

by

**Christine Petersen and
David Petersen**

Children's Press®

A Division of Scholastic Inc.

New York Toronto London Auckland Sydney
Mexico City New Delhi Hong Kong
Danbury, Connecticut

Woman in traditional Cuban clothing

Content Consultant
Thomas M. Davies, Jr., Ph.D.
*Professor of History;
Director, Center for Latin
American Studies;
Chair, Latin American Studies;
San Diego State University*

Reading Consultant
Nanci R. Vargus, Ed.D.
*Primary Multiage Teacher
Decatur Township Schools,
Indianapolis, IN*

*The photograph on the cover
shows Cathedral Plaza in
Havana. The photograph on
the title page shows cropland
in the Viñales Valley
of western Cuba.*

Library of Congress Cataloging-in-Publication Data

Petersen, Christine, and David Petersen.
Cuba / by Christine Petersen.
    p. cm. — (A true book)
    Includes bibliographical references and index.
    ISBN 0-516-22257-0 (lib.bdg.)   0-516-27358-2 (pbk.)
    1. Cuba—Juvenile literature. [1. Cuba.] I. Petersen, Christine. II. Title.
III. Series.
    F1758.5 .P48 2001
    972.91—dc21   00-057039

Contents

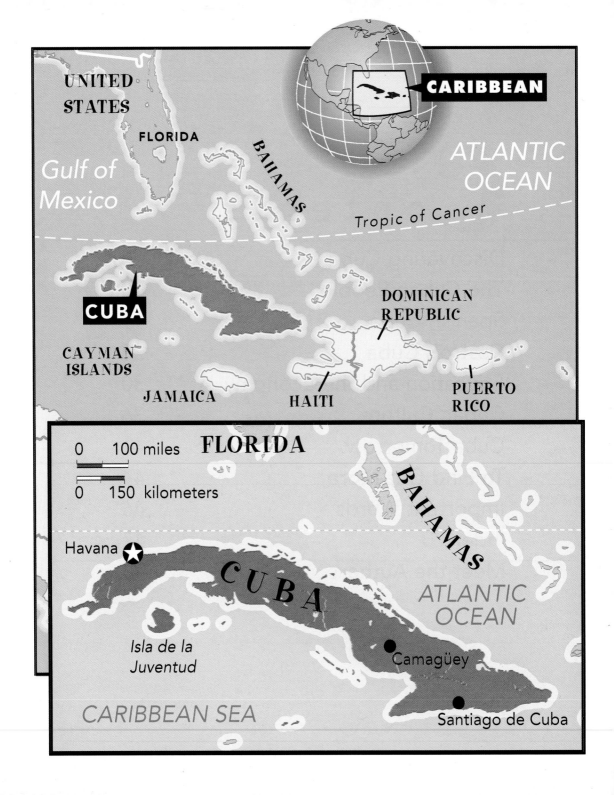

UNITED STATES

FLORIDA

Gulf of Mexico

BAHAMAS

CARIBBEAN

ATLANTIC OCEAN

Tropic of Cancer

CUBA

CAYMAN ISLANDS

DOMINICAN REPUBLIC

JAMAICA

HAITI

PUERTO RICO

FLORIDA

0   100 miles

0   150 kilometers

BAHAMAS

Havana ⭐

C U B A

ATLANTIC OCEAN

Isla de la Juventud

Camagüey

CARIBBEAN SEA

Santiago de Cuba

Discovering Cuba

The beautiful, tropical Republic of Cuba lies just 90 miles (145 kilometers) south of Florida. This island country is at the crossroads of North America, Central America, the Gulf of Mexico, the Caribbean Sea, and the Atlantic Ocean.

Cuba is the largest island in the Caribbean Sea. The

An overhead view of Cuban coastline (above) and one of Cuba's many beautiful beaches (right)

Republic of Cuba includes this large island and more than 1,600 other small islands.

Most people live along Cuba's lengthy coast. Even though Cuba is about 775 mi. (1,247 km) long, there are 3,570 mi. (5,745 km) of coastline. In this semi-tropical climate, children can go swimming almost all year long.

Three major mountain areas cover one-fourth of Cuba. In western Cuba is the Cordillera de Guaniguanico mountain area. It includes the Sierra de los Organos, where the unique *mogotes* are located. These large, steep, flat-topped mountains come straight out of the ground! Tobacco fields surround many of these limestone humps.

Cropland and *mogotes* in the Viñales Valley of western Cuba (above) and horses grazing in eastern Cuba (right)

The Sierra de Trinidad mountain range crosses central Cuba. In the east, the Sierra Maestra stretches for 150 miles (241 km).

Havana

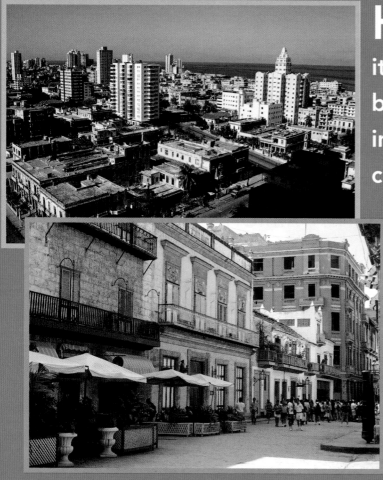

Havana, Cuba's capital city, was founded by Spanish colonists in 1515. Today the city is a mix of centuries-old colonial buildings and modern skyscrapers. Many buildings are painted in pastels, adding a touch of color.

Havana is home to more than 2 million people, but automobile traffic is light, because few Cubans own cars. Buses are free, and bicycles are everywhere.

The Cuban People

More than 11 million people live in Cuba. They all speak Spanish. But many people are not of Spanish origin. Cuba's interesting mix of ethnic groups reflects the history of the island.

In 1492, Christopher Columbus, exploring for Spain, became the first European to visit Cuba.

Cuban school children (above) and Cubans on a Saturday morning in the town of Sancti Spíritus (right)

Other Spanish explorers, soldiers, and settlers followed. Some of the native Cuban women had children by Spanish fathers. This mix of native Cuban and Spanish heritage is called *mestizo*.

Today about a quarter of Cubans are mestizo. The mestizos are the only Cubans with native "Indian" ancestors. The original Cubans, the ones Columbus called Indians, all died during the 1500s. Some were killed by the Spanish *conquistadors* (conquerors).

Others died of diseases the Spanish settlers brought with them. The rest died after being enslaved and mistreated by the Spanish owners of Cuban gold mines and sugar plantations.

After the native Indians had died, the Spanish plantation owners needed more people

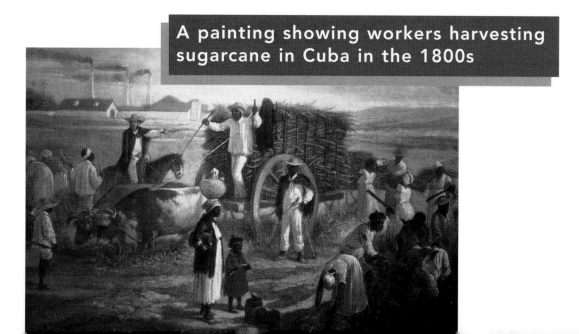

A painting showing workers harvesting sugarcane in Cuba in the 1800s

Many Cubans are of African ancestry.

to work in the sugarcane fields. They brought slaves from West Africa. Today, about one-third of Cubans are of Spanish-African or African ancestry.

In the late 1800s, thousands of Chinese workers came to Cuba. Most eventually settled in Havana. Today, about 1 percent of Cuba's population is of Chinese ancestry.

When the Spanish came to Cuba, they brought the Roman Catholic religion with them. Today, about 40 percent of Cubans are Roman Catholic. Yet Roman Catholicism never took hold as strongly in Cuba as it did in many other Latin

Worshipers at a Catholic Church service in Havana

American countries. Even as far back as the 1500s, Spanish Catholic missionaries had difficulty converting the Cuban people.

Later, the African slaves resisted because they associated the

Catholic religion with their mean owners. To keep their owners happy, many slaves disguised their African gods as Christian saints. This Afro-Cuban religion, called Santería, is based on the

A Santería ceremony (above) and religious altar (right)

Yoruba culture of West Africa. Santerían gods, called *Orishas*, may resemble Christian saints, but they are very different. Santería ceremonies include drums and dancing.

More than 50 percent of Cubans are not part of any religious group. After 1959, the Cuban government discouraged organized religion. Now Cubans are once again being allowed to join churches. More people are going to Catholic masses.

Spanish Cuba

In 1492, Christopher Columbus thought Cuba was "the most beautiful land that human eyes had ever seen." He claimed the land for Spain. The Spanish ruled Cuba for almost 400 years.

Many Cubans did not want to be part of Spain. In the late 1800s, José Martí wrote poems

The Spanish ruled Cuba for almost 400 years.

and gave speeches to encourage the Cuban people to fight for independence. They fought long and hard. In 1898, the United States joined the Cubans in their fight. After the Americans won, the Cubans made peace with Spain.

Cuban independence fighters in 1896 (above) and a statue honoring José Martí, the hero of Cuban independence (left)

From 1898 until 1902, the United States governed Cuba. After 1902, Cubans elected their own government, but the United States still influenced what happened.

Fulgencio Batista took over in 1933. He was a dictator who

Cuban dictator
Fulgencio Batista

would not tolerate anyone who thought things could be different or better. A few Cubans and wealthy businessmen from the United States owned most of the farms and businesses. Most of them did not care how the average Cuban was doing. Batista did not care either.

Castro's Cuba

Many Cubans did not want Batista to be their president. A young Cuban named Fidel Castro thought Batista would not improve things for his country. Castro got together with other disappointed and angry Cubans. They formed a rebel group.

In the 1950s, rebel leader Fidel Castro worked to overthrow the Batista government.

On July 26, 1953, Fidel Castro fired the first shots in a war against Batista. Castro and his supporters were captured and put in jail.

In 1956, Castro tried again to get rid of Batista. Finally, in

1959, they were able to over-throw Batista's government.

Fidel Castro became the president. Castro is a communist. Communists believe that the government should own almost everything. Most people work for the government, and personal freedom is limited.

The government promises the people that they will be treated fairly and have their basic needs met. It provides health care, child care, and education for everybody. But the government does not allow much disagreement. When Castro runs for re-election, no one is allowed to oppose him.

The United States does not approve of communism. Many American businessmen were angry when Castro made them leave Cuba and leave their businesses. The United States decided to stop trading with Cuba. Castro then turned to the communist Soviet Union for help. This made Cuba even less

President Castro and Soviet leader Nikita Khrushchev shake hands after signing an economic treaty in 1965.

popular in the United States. Decades later, the conflict between Cuba and the United States continues.

In the 1990s, Cuba faced very hard times. Many communist countries had collapsed and could not help. There was not enough food or fuel to go around. There was not enough money to provide the kind of schooling and health care people had depended on.

Not everybody liked the direction Cuba had taken. During the

In the 1990s, food shortages in Cuba forced the government to ration food.

Because of the U.S. trade embargo, Cubans cannot easily buy cars. Most cars in Cuba are old American cars built before 1960. Cubans take great care of their cars and have found creative ways to keep them running.

last 50 years, some Cubans have left their country. They were sad to go, but they wanted opportunities unavailable in their own country.

Education and the Economy

Education is very important in Cuba. When Castro became president, many people could not read. Now more than 95 percent of all Cubans can read and write!

In 1961, the Cuban government began to improve education for everyone by making

Cuban schoolchildren proudly holding up their artwork

schools more equal. Castro sent out an "army" of "reading soldiers" to educate the people. Private schools were abolished; now all children had to go to public school.

Today, Cuban children must go to school until they are twelve years old. Many finish high school. College is free and open to everyone who has demonstrated ability.

After students graduate, the government tells them where they must go to work. This is how the college students repay their country for their free education.

All schoolchildren must also work. Sometimes high-school students go to school for only half the day and learn a trade during the other half.

Cuban high-school students may learn skills ranging from bicycle assembly (left) to computer programming (right).

What kinds of work do Cubans do? They have many of the same jobs as other people in North America and Latin America. They are teachers, nurses, doctors, librarians, soldiers, builders, farmers, factory workers, and fishermen.

Cuba has few businesspeople because the communist government does not encourage private businesses. This is slowly changing. The Cuban government has also been allowing more foreign investment in order to make the economy stronger. About 76 percent of Cubans still work for the Cuban government.

One-fourth of Cuba's people work on farms. Cuba's major products are sugar, citrus fruit,

A Cuban fisherman with a catch of lobster (left) and workers at a Cuban grapefruit farm (below)

coffee, tobacco, and the country's world-famous cigars. Over half of working Cubans are in service jobs, many in the growing tourist industry. The remaining one-fourth work in industries.

Cuban Culture

Cuba provides many opportunities for artistic expression. Young children who show artistic promise are selected for special schools. Artists, dancers, musicians, and writers earn a good living.

Cuban music is enjoyed throughout the world. West

A rumba dancer and band in Havana

African rhythms and percussion instruments combine with Spanish *flamenco* sounds and guitars to create a unique sound. *Son*, Cuba's native dance music, goes back over 200 years. Some variations, such as the *rumba*, *mambo*, and *cha-cha-cha*, swept the world in the 1940s and 1950s.

Now many Cubans dance to popular salsa music. Jazz provides another unique blend of the Afro-Cuban musical heritage.

The most important Cuban foods are *moros y cristianos*—black beans and rice. Other basic foods include *yuca* (cassava), *boniato* (sweet potato), and *malanga* (a root vegetable), as well as citrus fruits such as grapefruit and oranges.

Garlic, peppers, and onions are common ingredients in

Moros y cristianos served with *platanos*, lobster, and avocado

Cuban food. Cubans eat eggs, chicken, and pork. Tropical fruits such as *platanos* (native bananas) are a favorite dessert.

Cubans love team sports, and baseball is a national passion. Children play baseball at school and at home. Talented young athletes are sent to special

Cuban kids playing baseball

baseball schools. Baseball is even helping to bring Cuba and the United States closer together. In 1999, Cuba's all-star team played the Baltimore Orioles in a series of exhibition games held in both countries.

Cuba Tomorrow

When the Soviet Union broke apart in 1991, Cuba lost its main trading partner. Life in Cuba became harder.

Yet Cuba remains a natural paradise filled with beautiful scenery. Foreign tourism is increasing. Visitors enjoy the world-famous food, music, and

dancing. Tourists might decide to tour historic Spanish buildings or relax on uncrowded beaches. Swimming, boating, and deep-sea fishing are popular activities.

Compared to its troubled past, Cuba's future is looking brighter. Everyone has government-

provided health care and child care. Most people can read and write. Education is available to everyone. Recently, Cubans were allowed to own small businesses. Change is in the air.

Cuba libre!

To Find Out More

Here are some additional resources to help you learn more about Cuba:

Books

Hallworth, Grace. **Down by the River: Afro-Caribbean Rhymes, Games and Songs.** Cartwheel Books, 1996.

Morrison, Marion. **Cuba** (Enchantment of the World). Children's Press, 1999.

Shalant, Phyllis. **Look What We've Brought You from the Caribbean: Crafts, Games, Recipes, Stories, and Other Cultural Activities.** Julian Messner, 1999.

Staub, Frank. **Children of Cuba.** Carolrhoda Books, 1996.

Organizations and Online Sites

The Cuban Experience
http://library.thinkquest.org /18355/

ThinkQuest's site is an excellent review of Cuban culture, history, politics, and people.

CubaWeb
http://www.cubaweb.cu/ Cub_ing/index.asp

Cuba's official website features stories from the Cuban press, plus information on investments, trade, science, medicine, culture, and tourism. It is set up in Spanish; click the word "English" on the upper-left corner to switch.

Fidel Castro Biography
http://cnn.com/resources/ newsmakers/world/ namerica/castro.html

CNN's online biography of the Cuban leader.

Photo Collection on Cuba
http://www.cubanet.org/ fotoindex.html

Photographs showing the people, architecture, and natural wonders of Cuba.

Important Words

ancestors relatives from the past

convert to change from one belief or religion to another

dictator person who rules absolutely

discourage to attempt to persuade not to to something

embargo policy by which a country refuses to trade with another country

heritage background

missionaries people sent to spread a religious faith among unbelievers

oppose to run against in an election

origin place where something comes from

percussion instrument musical instrument sounded by striking

ration to give out in small portions

resemble to look or appear to be like

tolerate to allow something to exist

Index

Meet the Authors

Christine Petersen grew up in coastal California and now lives in the lake country near Minneapolis, Minnesota. Christine is a biologist and educator who has spent years researching and lecturing about North American bats. She likes to hike and snowshoe, read good books, play with her two cats, and travel.

David Petersen is Christine Petersen's father. In various former lives, David has been a Marine Corps helicopter pilot, a mailman, a college teacher, and a magazine editor. Today, David lives in a little cabin on a big mountain in Colorado with his wife, Caroline, and two big dogs. David's passions are studying and writing about nature.

Photographs ©: Bridgeman Art Library International Ltd., London/New York: 13 (Index); Corbis-Bettmann: 40 (AFP), 1 (Richard Bickel), 21 right (Hulton-Deutsch Collection), 8 bottom, 17 bottom (Robert van der Hilst), 35 left (Arne Hodalic), 17 top (Francoise de Mulder), 20 (Historical Picture Archive), 22, 24; Impact Visuals/Mario Tapia: 28; International Stock Photo/ Greg Johnston: 21 left; Liaison Agency, Inc.: 27 (Hulton Getty), 9 bottom (Mark Lewis); Nik Wheeler: 35 right; South American Pictures: 39 (Jason P. Howe), 11 bottom, 31 (Tony Morrison), 9 top, 12, 14, 37 (Rolando Pujol); Stone: cover, 6 bottom, 43 (Mark Lewis), 2 (Robert Frerck), 6 top (Donald Nausbaum), 29 top (Lorne Resnick), 29 bottom (Trevor Wood); The Image Works: 33 left (L. Dematteis), 16 (D. Harse), 8 top (Marcel & Eva Malherbe), 11 top, 33 right (Mel Rosenthal), 42 (Bob Strong). Map by Joe LeMonnier.